A New True Book

OPOSSUMS

By Emilie U. Lepthien

CHILDRENS PRESS®

CHICAGO

Opossum babies clinging to a branch

Project Editor: Fran Dyra
Design: Margrit Fiddle

Library of Congress Cataloging-in-Publication Data

Lepthien, Emilie U. (Emilie Utteg)
  Opossums / by Emilie U. Lepthien.
    p.   cm.–(A New true book)
  Includes index.
  ISBN 0-516-01055-7
  1. Opossums–Juvenile literature. [1.   Opossums.]
I.   Title.
QL737.M34L45   1994
599.2–dc20   93-33516
                                        CIP
                                        AC

PHOTO CREDITS

American Society of Mammalogists, Mammal Slide Library, © Philip Myers–Neg #484, 36 (left), Neg #485, 36 (inset)

Animals Animals–© Stouffer Productions, 20; © R.K. LaVal, 38; © Hans & Judy Beste, 40

AUSCAPE–© Mike W. Gillam, 42

© Erwin and Peggy Bauer–8 (top), 14 (left), 26 (left)

© Alan & Sandy Carey–Cover, 23

Dembinsky Photo Associates–© Gary Meszaros, 29

Photo Courtesy of National Museum of the American Indian, Smithsonian Institution–Neg #39684, 44

Photri–© Blakesley, 17; © Leonard Lee Rue III, 27, 30

Root Resources–© Jim Nachel, 16

Tom Stack & Associates–© Don and Esther Phillips, 2; © John Cancalosi, 5; © Thomas Kitchin, 9 (left); © Joe & Carol McDonald, 19; © Dave Watts, 22

© Lynn M. Stone–15

Tony Stone Images–© Gay Bumgarner, 12; © Leonard Lee Rue III, 32; © Fritz Prenzel, 39 (right)

SuperStock International, Inc.–© Leonard Lee Rue III, 45

Valan–© James D. Markou, 6, 25; © Robert C. Simpson, 8 (left); © Wayne Lankinen, 8 (right); © Aubrey Lang, 9 (right); © Bob & Melissa Simpson, 11; © John Cancalosi, 14 (top & bottom right), 39 (left); © Michel Bourque, 18

Visuals Unlimited–© D. Newman, 26 (right); © Kjell B. Sandred, 34

COVER: Opossum

TABLE OF CONTENTS

PLAYING POSSUM

Have you ever "played possum"? If you have, you probably curled up in a ball and pretended you were asleep.

The opossum uses this trick to save its life when it is attacked. The

"Playing possum." When the opossum curls up
and lies still, its enemies think it is dead.

opossum lies very still. Its
body is curled, and its
eyes and mouth are partly
open. Its legs stiffen, and
its heartbeat slows down.

The opossum quickly "comes back to life" when the enemy leaves.

In a short time, the attacker thinks the opossum is dead and loses interest. When the enemy leaves, the opossum recovers.

The opossum has another trick as well. Its first defense when attacked is to release a liquid that gives off a strong odor. The smell drives some attackers away.

The enemies of opossums
include raccoons (top), great
horned owls (left), and mink (above).

The red fox (left) and the coyote (right) may also kill opossums.

In spite of their clever ways, however, opossums rarely live more than two years. They have many natural enemies—owls, coyotes, raccoons, minks, dogs, foxes, and humans.

9

THE HUMAN FACTOR

Every year thousands of opossums are killed by cars and trucks. More are killed by hunters.

In the southern United States, opossums are hunted in late fall and winter. Hunters go out at

A hunter and his dog. Hunters go out at night to track opossums.

night with dogs and flashlights. The dogs "tree" the possums (chase them up a tree) so that the hunters can capture them.

Opossums sometimes damage the crops in

11

A young opossum investigates a cherry tomato plant.

sugarcane fields and in banana and mango groves. But most farmers know that opossums help them by keeping down the insect population.

MARSUPIALS

Opossums are marsupials. Marsupials are mammals that have a pouch in which their young nurse and grow after birth.

There are about 250 species of marsupials in

The wallaroo (left), the wombat (top), and the Tasmanian devil (above) are some of the many Australian marsupials.

North America, South America, Australia, and the islands of Southeast Asia.

There are at least 65 different species of opossum in North, Central,

14

and South America. The common, or Virginia, opossum is the only marsupial that lives throughout much of the United States and southeastern Canada.

The Virginia opossum

The opossum has a white face and a pink nose.
Its ears and tail make it look like a big rat.

APPEARANCE

The common opossum looks like it has forgotten to comb its thick, grayish-white fur. Its nose is kept moist by glands that give off an oil.

Opossums have 50 teeth—more than any other North American mammal. Like dogs and cats, their teeth are adapted for slashing and tearing food.

The opossum's fifty teeth are adapted to eating a wide variety of foods.

The opossum's hind foot has a thumb-like big toe.
Strong nails grow on the other four toes.

SPECIAL FEET AND TAILS

Opossums have five toes on each foot. They can use the toes on their forefeet like fingers.

The hind foot has a thumb-like big toe. There are nails instead of claws on the other four toes. The big toe and the nails help the opossum grasp things and climb trees.

Opossums have a long, prehensile tail without much hair on it. A

The end of an opossum's prehensile tail can curl around and grasp tree branches.

Young opossums can hang by their tail from a tree
branch, but adults are usually too heavy to do this.

prehensile tail can wrap tightly around and grasp a tree branch. The tail can be used like a "fifth hand" when the opossum is moving about in the trees. Young opossums can hang by their tail from a branch.

SIZE AND WEIGHT

The pygmy possum
of Australia
is about the
size of a mouse.

The pygmy possum is small. But the common, or Virginia, opossum is the size of a big cat. Its body measures from 12 to almost 20 inches (30.5 to

22

The Virginia opossum is the size of a big cat.

50 cm) long. The tail may be 10 to 21 inches (25.5 to 53.5 cm) long. Generally, they weigh 4 to 9 pounds (2 to 4 kg). Older opossums may weigh up to 12 pounds (5.5 kg). Opossums continue to grow throughout their lifetime.

ADAPTING
TO A NEW LIFE

When European settlers
built towns and farms in
North America, the homes
of many wild animals were
destroyed. Most animals
that lose their habitat
become endangered or
threatened species. But
not the opossum. It has
found ways to adapt to
life even in the city.

Opossums usually live in
trees. They prefer to live

Opossums like to live in woodlands, where they can find places for dens and lots of food.

in woodlands along rivers. But they also live in fields and on mountainsides–almost anywhere except deserts.

Opossums hunt at night. Their sense of smell helps them find food. They eat almost anything, including garbage. They can easily

Opossums spend much of their time
looking for food. They can climb
onto the small branches of fruit trees.
In towns, they raid garbage cans.

turn over garbage cans
with their front feet.

In the wild, their diet
includes grass, mushrooms,
fruits, insects, birds' eggs,
chickens, and even
poisonous snakes. Opossums
are immune to the venom
of rattlesnakes.

HOMES AND FAMILIES

A hollow log makes a good den for an opossum.

Opossums sleep through much of the day. However, they do not hibernate, or sleep through the winter.

They make a den in a hollow log or in a hole under the root or stump of a tree. Sometimes they live in an abandoned squirrel's nest high in a tree.

After the male and female mate, the female

carries her young inside her for only 11 to 12 days. She then gives birth to as many as 18 to 25 babies—each smaller than a honeybee.

The babies can neither see nor hear. They have no fur. Their hind legs are useless. But they must find their way up into the mother's pouch to nurse. And they must hurry. There are only thirteen nipples, or teats, in the pouch—not enough for all the babies.

These baby opossums have made the journey
into their mother's pouch.

Using special claws on
their front feet, they pull
themselves up to and into
the pouch.

As soon as a baby
finds a nipple, it hangs on
tight and begins nursing.

Baby opossums fastened to nipples in their mother's pouch

The babies stay in the pouch from six weeks to two months. They do not let go of the nipple during that time.

As the babies grow, the pouch becomes very crowded. The babies are safe inside. But the air they breathe—and rebreathe—has eight to ten times the normal amount of carbon dioxide. Usually, only about seven in the litter survive.

After two months, the babies leave the pouch. They look very much like adult opossums, but they still need their mother to provide food and safety.

Eight-week-old opossums ride on their mother's back.

The young opossums climb up on their mother's back and hold on to her fur with their front feet. Some of the young wrap their tails around their mother's tail and hang on for a ride. They often try to crowd back into the pouch for a short time.

The mother teaches her young to catch and eat insects, small rodents, and birds' eggs. They stay with their mother until they are old enough to take care of themselves—about three months. Three to five months later, they are full-grown adults.

In Canada, opossums breed only once a year, in the spring. In the southern United States, they may have two or even three litters a year.

STRANGE ANIMALS

Some marsupial relatives of the common opossum carry their young between two flaps of skin under their bellies. Most, however, have a pouch with an opening at the front.

The water opossum lives in Mexico and South America. It is the only opossum that has adapted to life in the water.

It makes its burrow in the bank of a river. At

The water opossum—also called the yapok—of South America is the only marsupial that lives partly in water. Its webbed feet (inset) help it to swim.

dusk, it comes out of its burrow to swim and catch food such as crayfish and shellfish. Water opossums eat their food on land.

The water opossum has webbed hind feet that help it swim. Its tail, which is much longer than its body, helps it move through the water.

Two weeks after water opossums mate, about five babies are born. They climb up into their mother's pouch, which is watertight.

The pouch has a strong ring of muscle that keeps it tightly closed even when the mother is in the water. The young stay dry, but no one knows how the babies in the pouch get enough oxygen to breathe.

THE MURINE OPOSSUMS

A Mexican mouse opossum scrambling across leaves

Murine opossums look like mice. They are native to Central and South America and spend most of their time in trees. The female has no pouch. After the young are born, they hang on to their mother's nipples.

THE MARSUPIALS OF AUSTRALIA

Wallabies, kangaroos, and koalas are Australia's most familiar marsupials. But other interesting marsupials also live in Australia.

Koalas (left) and kangaroos (right) are some well-known marsupials of Australia.

This squirrel-sized marsupial is found in the woodlands of
eastern Australia. Its long, furry tail helps the animal
keep its balance while gliding.

The lesser-known gliding opossum of Australia has a 12-inch (30.5-cm) body and an 18-inch (46-cm) tail. A flap of skin stretches along each side between its legs. This opossum can glide up to 180 feet (55 m) from one tree to another.

Marsupial moles live in Australia's remote desert areas. Their tiny eyes have neither lenses nor pupils. They spend much of their time underground.

The marsupial mole can

Marsupial moles eat earthworms and other small animals that live in the soil.

dig a hole with the horny shield on its muzzle. It digs a tunnel with its forepaws and throws the dirt back under its body. Then its hind feet kick the dirt farther back. It continues to fill up the tunnel behind itself. Finally it comes up to the surface.

The female's pouch opens to the rear. She has only two nipples, so she cannot raise a large litter.

ANCIENT ANIMALS

Scientists have found fossils showing that marsupials lived on Earth 60 million years ago. In North America, the Algonquian Indians called them *apasum*, meaning "white beast." The Ojibwa name for them—*wabasim*—meant "white dog."

An early Native American pottery jar in the shape of an opossum.

It is easy to see why
we call them "opossum,"
and why scientists
continue to study these
fascinating mammals.

WORDS YOU SHOULD KNOW

abandon (uh • BAN • dun)—to leave behind; to go away from

burrow (BER • oh)—a hole that an animal digs in the ground to make a home

carbon dioxide (KAR • bun dye • OX • ide)—a gas in the air that is made up of carbon and oxygen

desert (DEH • zert)—an area of land that gets little rainfall and has very dry soil

endangered (en • DAIN • jerd)—in danger of dying out

gland (GLAND)—a special body part that makes substances the body uses or gives off

habitat (HAB • ih • tat)—home; the place where an animal usually lives

hibernate (HYE • ber • nait)—to sleep through the winter

lens (LENZ)—a clear part of the eye that focuses light rays

litter (LIT • er)—a group of baby animals born at the same time to the same mother

mammal (MAM • ill)—one of a group of warm-blooded animals that have hair and nurse their young with milk

mango (MANG • goh)—a fruit with a thick, orange rind

marsupial (mar • SOO • pea • il)—a mammal that nurses its young in a pouch

murine (MYOO • ryne)—like a mouse

oxygen (AHX • ih • jin)—a gas found in the air that humans and animals need to breathe

poisonous (POY • zun • uss)—containing poison; causing sickness or death

population (pah • pyoo • LAY • shun)—the total number of animals of the same kind living at the same time

prehensile (pre • HEN • sil)—able to wrap around and grasp objects

pupil (PYOO • pil)–the opening in the middle of the colored part of an eye

rodent (ROH • duhnt)–an animal, such as a rat or squirrel, that has long, sharp front teeth for gnawing

species (SPEE • sheez)–a group of related plants or animals that are able to interbreed

tunnel (TUH • nil)–a hole that makes a path down through the ground

venom (VEH • num)–the poison of some snakes, spiders, etc.

webbed (WEBD)–having the toes joined by wide pieces of skin

INDEX

About the Author

Emilie U. Lepthien received her BA and MS degrees and certificate in school administration from Northwestern University. She taught upper-grade science and social studies, wrote and narrated science programs for the Chicago Public Schools' station WBEZ, and was principal in Chicago, Illinois, for twenty years. She received the American Educator's Medal from Freedoms Foundation.

She is a member of Delta Kappa Gamma Society International, Chicago Principals' Association, Illinois Women's Press Association, National Federation of Press Women, and AAUW.

She has written books in the Enchantment of the World, New True Books, and America the Beautiful series.